Interfacings

Carry-Along Reference Guide

Kristine Poor

Landauer Publishing

Copyright © 2019 by Kristine Poor and Landauer Publishing,
www.landauerpub.com, an imprint of Fox Chapel Publishing Company, Inc.,
903 Square Street, Mount Joy, PA 17552.
978-1-947163-26-3
Printed in China

Contents

Introduction

What is interfacing? Interfacing is the layer of fabric between the outer garment or project and the lining or facing. It shapes, supports, and stabilizes. Most projects last longer and look more professional with suitable interfacing.

Choosing and using interfacings properly makes such a difference in the outcome of your project. Use this guide to help you get started in the world of interfacings.

How Do You Choose?

The pattern supply list should serve as a guide to choosing interfacing. It is good to know why a certain interfacing has been recommended, especially when you want to get creative and start using fabrics other than what has been suggested.

There are three main types of interfacing:
1. Woven—This interfacing is produced just like fabric and is generally more durable than a nonwoven.
2. Nonwoven—This type of interfacing is made from polyester fibers bonded together to form a fabric. It will exhibit little or no shrinkage and will not ravel.
3. Knit—This soft interfacing has stretch and can be used with both woven and knit fabrics.

General Tips

TESTING YOUR INTERFACING

Because there are no right or wrong answers when choosing interfacing, it is always best to test before you get started. This will ensure that you get the result that you want.

COLOR

There are dark interfacings as well as light. In some cases when using a dark fabric, light interfacing may show through (and vice versa), so this is something to consider when choosing your interfacing.

DRAPE OR STIFFNESS

There are lightweight to heavyweight interfacings on the market. The more support you need, the stiffer the interfacing. Try this at the store: Lay your fabric over the interfacing—are you getting the result that you want? Try different weights until you are satisfied with your choice.

FUSIBLE VS. SEW-IN APPLICATION

Choosing between a fusible and a sew-in interfacing depends on personal preference, the fabric, and the degree of firmness desired. Fusible interfacing has a layer of heat-activated adhesive that is either printed or sprayed on the interfacing and can be a great time saver. They can also make a fabric slightly crisper than a sew-in interfacing of comparable weight. If you are unsure whether your fabric can be fused, ask the fabric retailer where you purchased the fabric, or if that is not possible, do a test with your fabric and interfacing.

Applying Fusible Interfacing

Always refer to the instructions that come with your interfacing. Use a press cloth when fusing to protect your fashion fabric. It can be a purchased press cloth or a piece of muslin or batiste. **Important!** Always protect your ironing surface (beneath the project) with parchment paper or a Teflon™ sheet.

For fusible interfacing to be applied to fabric properly, you need to control three things:

- Time
- Temperature
- Pressure

Always PRESS—do not iron in a gliding motion! Fuse from the center then move out to the outer edges. The fusible glue needs time to activate. Press about 10–20 seconds on each section, and then lift and position in the next section, overlapping as you go. **Note:** Hand-held steamers will *not* bond interfacing to fabric.

Try this: Use a damp press cloth as a timing tool. The cloth will be dry after 10–20 seconds of fusing. If not, turn up the temperature on the iron and press a little longer.

Let the fabric cool for at least five minutes. Test the bond by attempting to peel the interfacing away from the fabric. The fusible interfacing should be secure. If it isn't, adjust the time or temperature and test again.

If the result is wrinkly or bubbled, lower the temperature and try again.

If you get no adhesion and notice a shiny surface on the fabric, the glue has transferred to the fabric. Lower the temperature and retest.

Applying Sewn-in Interfacing

Sew a scrap of interfacing to a scrap of the fashion fabric as directed in the project instructions. Use a washable fabric glue stick to temporarily hold the interfacing in place.

When finished, ask yourself the following questions: Is the fabric supported as you would expect? Is the fabric too stiff? Play with different weights to achieve the look that you want.

COMBINATIONS

Sometimes a single interfacing is not enough—you might need a combination of more than one interfacing to achieve the look and function that you need. Make sure that you test beforehand so that you know what to expect when making your project.

Care and Storage

CARE

Be sure to note the care instructions of the interfacings when you purchase them. Select interfacings that require the same care as the project fabric. (Use washable interfacings with washable fabrics; likewise, with dry-clean-only fabrics and interfacings.) If you are unsure of the care instructions for the fabric or the interfacing, wash a test sample to check the results.

To pre-shrink fusible interfacing (and avoid any unwanted results later), fill a sink with warm water (do not add detergent). Soak for about ten minutes. Gently squeeze out excess water by rolling in a clean, dry towel and lay flat to dry.

STORAGE

Fusible interfacing should not be stored for long periods of time; adhesives can be affected by light, moisture, and heat. Make sure to test a sample of older material before use.

Using This Guide

There are so many interfacings available right now that I could not possibly list each one. I listed just a few examples in each category to get you started.

When you find an interfacing that you like to use, keep a sample of it in a notebook, along with the manufacturer's instructions and the name of the project that you used it on. You'll be glad you did!

Guide

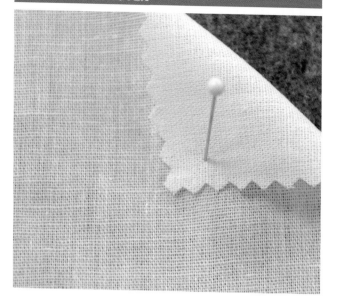

Product/Type
Woven interfacing, sew-in or fusible

Characteristics
Woven interfacing, like fabric, has a warp (lengthwise) and a weft (crosswise). It's generally more durable than nonwoven. The fusible version tends to produce less wrinkles and dimples than nonwoven fusible interfacings.

Fiber Content
100% cotton, cotton and poly blend, or 100% polyester

- Pellon® SF101 Shape-Flex® Woven Fusible Interfacing
- HTC Form Flex Fusible Interfacing
- Bosal Fashion Fuse Woven Interfacing
- HTC Sta-Form Durable Press
- HTC Touch O'Gold II
- HTC Veri-Shape

Uses or Tasks

Woven interfacing adds stability and body to garments, crafts, quilts, and bags. This interfacing moves in the same way as the fashion fabric. Tailored collars, cuffs, and facings in fine garments are generally interfaced with woven interfacing due to its superior drape. This interfacing is a great choice to add to bag linings that will see daily wear.

Tips

- Use sew-in interfacing for those fabrics that can't be fused.
- Align the grain of the fashion fabric with the grain of the woven interfacing when constructing garments. This is done to maintain the look and drape of the fabric in the garment.
- If you find that your test piece is too stiff, cut your interfacing on the bias to soften the drape while also providing support.
- Use a woven interfacing as a backing for needlework and punch embroidery.
- Use a small piece of woven interfacing behind buttons and buttonholes to maintain shape in that area.

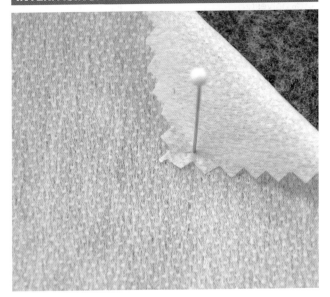

Product/Type
Nonwoven interfacing, sew-in or fusible

Characteristics
A layer of fibers bonded together and compressed to mimic fabric. This type of interfacing resembles a dryer sheet. It provides allover stability (non-directional), and does not ravel or lose its shape.

The adhesive in the fusible nonwoven interfacing can be either "printed" (dots) or laminated (a fine layer of fusible web applied) onto the interfacing at the factory.

Fiber Content
100% polyester

Limited List of Brand Names
- HTC Fusi-Form (lightweight and suit weight)
- HTC Intra-Face (featherweight, lightweight, medium weight, and heavyweight)
- HTC Sheer D'Light (featherweight, lightweight, and medium weight)
- Pellon 845F Designer's Lite™
- Pellon 855F Tailor's Elite™
- Pellon 880F Sof-Shape®
- Pellon 881F Pel-Aire™
- Pellon 950F ShirTailor®

- Pellon ES114 Easy-Shaper®
- Pellon 900 Series Fusible Interfacings, various weights
- Bosal 334 Fusible Non-Woven Medium All-Purpose Dura Fuse

Uses or Tasks

Nonwoven interfacings are generally less expensive than their woven counterparts. They do not drape as well as woven interfacings, so they should be reserved for areas that require crisper shaping. Nonwoven interfacing can be used in garments, crafts, quilts, and home décor.

Fusible interfacings are easy to work with; once pieces are fused together, they can be treated as a single unit.

Tips

- Fabrics treated with soil and water-resistant coatings are also resistant to fusing. In this case, choose a nonwoven sew-in for stability and body. Heat-sensitive fabrics (metallic, textured, and beaded fabrics) may require sew-ins as well.
- If not fused properly, some fusible interfacings can separate and cause ugly bubbles. Bubbles can happen if the temperature of the iron is too high during the fusing process, or too much moisture is used. Never completely soak your interfacing or press cloth; use a damp press cloth or a fine mist of water.

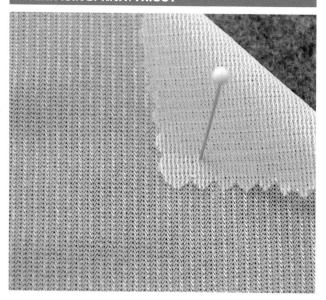

Product/Type

Knit/tricot interfacing, sew-in or fusible; also available with warp (lengthwise)–insertions or weft (crosswise)–insertions

Characteristics

This is a stretch knit/tricot interfacing that's used for adding structure to knits and woven fabrics. They can be sew-in or fusible.

Fiber Content

100% polyester

Limited List of Brand Names

- Bosal 328 Fusible Tricot
- Bosal 332 Sheer Fusible Tricot
- Bosal 351 Soft Stretch Fusible Tricot Interfacing
- Pellon EK 130 Easy-Knit™
- HTC Armo Weft
- HTC Fusi-Knit
- HTC So-Sheer
- HTC Sof-Knit
- HTC Textured Weft
- HTC Whisper Weft
- Pellon 860F Ultra Weft™
- Pellon 865F Bi-Stretch Lite™
- Pellon SK135 Sheer-Knit™

Uses or Tasks

Knit/tricot interfacings are soft and stretchy, giving the fabric a softer drape. They also add structure and stability to knit and woven fabrics. They're also ideal for adding structure to sheer fabrics, great for adding neckline facings to knits, and can be used to underline scratchy fabrics to provide a smooth lining.

Knit interfacings with a weft- or warp-insertion are actually tricot with an extra yarn inserted in a warp or weft direction for added stability. The weft-insertion has the most stretch on the bias. The warp-insertions have the most stretch in the crosswise direction, since it is inserted using a chevron pattern.

Tips

- ▪ Making a T-shirt quilt? Use knit interfacing to add stability while still preserving the texture of the T-shirt.
- ▪ Always do a test fuse with stretch interfacings. (Follow the manufacturer's instructions.) Start with a lower temperature on your iron and test. If you find that the bond is not sufficient, increase the temperature and retest.
- ▪ Test the grain of the knit interfacing—some interfacing has one-way stretch; others have more.

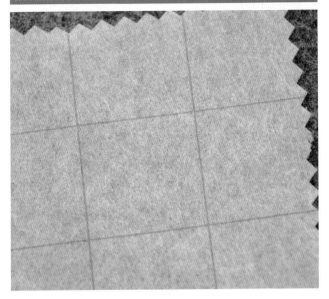

Product/Type
Quilter's grids, fusible

Characteristics
This is a nonwoven fusible interfacing printed with grid
lines for precision piecing when using it with quilts and
quilted projects.

Fiber Content
100% polyester

Limited List of Brand Names

- Bosal 427 Quilter's Grid Series, 1" and 2½" (2.5 and 6.4cm) grids in horizontal and diagonal format
- Pellon 820 Quilter's Grid™, 1" (2.54cm) printed grids in horizontal and diagonal format
- Pellon 821 Quilter's Grid On-Point™, 1" (2.54cm) printed grids on-point
- Quiltsmart (there are a variety of preprinted grids and projects)

Uses or Tasks

This is a light nonwoven fusible interfacing. Place the fusible side *up* on your ironing surface. Arrange the fabric squares on top of the grid and fuse. Stitch according to the pattern instructions.

Tips

- Make sure to leave no extra interfacing hanging out on the outer edges of your project—it will gum up your iron.
- Test the fusing before starting your project to determine the correct iron settings.
- As you fuse, be careful to not move your fabric pieces (lift up vertically after pressing and don't "iron").
- Sew as directed on your pattern—you may want to use a walking foot to prevent shifting.

Product/Type
Buckram, sew-in or fusible

Characteristics
Crisp, cotton woven used mainly for stiffening fabrics used for hats, drapery headers, costumes—anything that needs to stand upright on its own. Buckram has a starched resin finish.

Fiber Content
100% cotton

- Pellon 375 Buckram Sew-In Interfacing
- Pellon 376 Fusible Buckram
- Bosal 370 Mid Weight Buckram Interfacing

Uses or Tasks

You can find buckram on the inside of a baseball hat, supporting the dense embroidery stitches. It adds flexible, durable support and body to your project. Please note: buckram is *not* machine washable.

Tips

- To shape or mold buckram, dampen it with a spray bottle of plain water. Smooth the prepared buckram over a shape that has been covered in plastic wrap, let dry, and cover with fabric.
- If you are making a heavily used item with buckram, it is advisable to spray it with a fabric protector—like Scotchgard™—to repel stains.

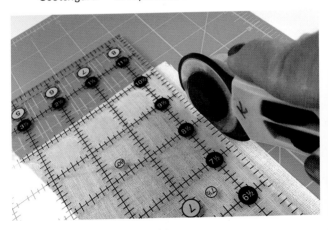

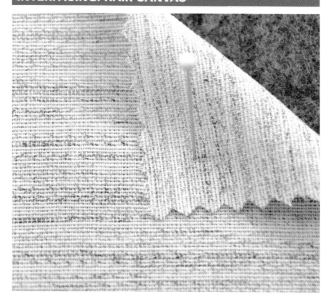

Product/Type
Hair canvas, sew-in or fusible

Characteristics
Sew-in and fusible hair canvas is a woven interfacing used with traditional tailoring methods. It is made with a blend of materials and generally contains goat hair or horsehair.

Fiber Content
Polyester, hair, cotton, and wool blend

Limited List of Brand Names
- Pellon HC110 Sew-In Hair Canvas
- Pellon HC120F Fusible Hair Canvas
- Bosal 340 Fusible Hair Canvas
- Bosal 341 Sew-in Hair Canvas
- HTC Acro (sew-in and fusible)
- HTC Tailor's Pride

Uses or Tasks

Hair canvas is found on the inside lapel and shoulders of fine-tailored garments. It produces a smoothly shaped garment with a strong structure and a more heavily constructed feel. A jacket made with hair canvas will last longer, as well.

Hair canvas can be steamed/pressed to add more shaping. It can also be used in bag making, where a sturdy interfacing is needed.

It is easy to sew and is machine washable but must be hung to dry.

Tips
- To preshrink hair canvas, completely iron the fabric on a wool setting with steam. Lay flat to dry.
- The method used in hand-tailoring hair canvas is pad stitching. This creates the garment silhouette.

Product/Type
Precuts for waistbands or purse straps

Characteristics
Woven and nonwoven, sew-in or fusible

Fiber Content
Various fiber content across brands

- Clover Create-a-Strap
- Staple Sewing Aids Ban-Rol Smooth Edge Waistband Material
- Dritz Perfect Waist Maker Fusible Interfacing

Uses or Tasks

For adding body to waistbands, the accurate cuts make these products a good choice for beginner sewers to achieve professional results. Some brands have perforated fold lines that make preparing and topstitching easier.

When making purse straps, extra-firm crisp edges can be easily achieved.

Tips

- Follow the manufacturer's instructions for the best results; these instructions will include the proper cutting widths for fashion fabric in addition to waistbands and purse straps.
- Some products can be used to create narrow hems.

Product/Type
Stabilizers for craft and home décor projects, sew-in
or fusible

Characteristics
This ultra-firm, resilient, and easy-to-cut nonwoven stiffener
is for use in projects such as bags, boxes, hat brims, fabric
bowls, or any other projects that require very firm, stable
support. This is a great option for crafts, home décor, and
embroidery projects. Products can be sew-in or fusible.

Fiber Content
Polyester

Limited List of Brand Names

- Pellon 809 Décor-Bond®
- Pellon 70 Peltex® Sew-In Ultra Firm Stabilizer
- Pellon 71F Peltex I One-Sided Fusible Ultra Firm Stabilizer
- Pellon 72F Peltex II Two-Sided Fusible Ultra Firm Stabilizer
- Bosal 336 Medium-Weight Craf-tex Lite
- Bosal 337 Non-Woven Heavyweight Craf-tex
- Bosal 436 Sew-In Non-Woven Medium-Weight Craf-tex Lite
- Bosal 437 Sew-In Non-Woven Heavyweight Craf-tex

Uses or Tasks

Use these stiffeners for bag bottoms, fabric boxes, tote bag straps, fabric bowls, and in Christmas ornaments.

Tips

- When using these stiffer products, consider a heavier needle (start with a size 90/14) so that the needle can handle the thickness. Experiment with Microtex (sharp), jeans, or topstitch needles. Always stitch a test sandwich with your fabric and stabilizer, ensuring that the test sample mimics the number of layers to be used.
- If the stiffener you purchased isn't fusible, apply fusible web to make your own fusible product.
- When stitching a heavy stabilizer into your project, it may be necessary to trim the stabilizer to eliminate bulk in the seams.

Product/Type
Decovil/Decovil light, fusible

Characteristics
This is a fusible nonwoven interfacing with a leather-like hand that is tear resistant, dimensionally stable, and easy to shape. Decovil light is lighter, softer, and thinner than Decovil.

Fiber Content
Polyester/viscose/polyamide

Limited List of Brand Names
- Pellon 526 Decovil
- Pellon 526 Decovil Light

Uses or Tasks
Decovil is a great choice for fashion accessories that require thin, firm support, like hats, belts, bags, and wallets. Great for fabric bowls and other home décor items.

Tips
- Make sure to test the product with your fashion fabric before sewing.
- Cut the piece of Decovil to the size of the piece you are stabilizing, minus the seam allowances. Fuse to the wrong side then stitch around the Decovil— but not *into* the Decovil—making sure that you have enough room to turn your piece to the right side. Keeping the Decovil out of the seam allowances will give you a nice smooth edge.
- Fuse Decovil to the wrong side of the fabric with the assistance of a damp press cloth. Press for about six seconds then lay flat to cool for approximately 30 minutes.
- Use binder clips in lieu of pins to keep the layers together.

Product/Type
Sew-in foam stabilizer

Characteristics
A very stable sheet foam interfacing that is stable, retains its shape, is durable, and does not degrade over time. Foam is thicker than its interfacing counterparts. May have a tricot layer on either side that grips the fabric and holds it in place.

Fiber Content
100% polyester

Limited List of Brand Names
- Bosal 492 In-R-Form Sew-In Foam Stabilizer
- ByAnnie Soft and Stable
- Pellon FF77 Flex-Foam™

Uses or Tasks
If you make bags, foam interfacing will ensure that your creations look polished and professional. They can also be used in home décor and craft projects.

Tips
- Use binder clips or Wonder Clips® when seaming pieces together to avoid pesky bent pins.
- If you are having trouble stitching, consider changing needles—try a Microtex (sharp), jeans, or topstitch needle.
- You can achieve a wonderful quilted texture with this product. If you are working on a project that needs quilting, mark it on the inside and quilt from that side.

Product/Type
Fusible foam stabilizer

Characteristics
A very stable sheet foam interfacing laminated with fusible adhesive on one or both sides. Like it's sew-in cousin, it is stable, retains its shape, is durable, and does not degrade over time. The single-sided version has a tricot layer on one side that grips the fabric and holds it in place.

Fiber Content
100% polyester

Limited List of Brand Names

- Bosal 493 In-R-Form Plus Double Sided Fusible Foam Stabilizer
- Bosal 495S In-R-Form Plus Single Sided Fusible Foam Stabilizer
- Pellon FF78 Flex-Foam Single-Sided Fusible
- Pellon FF79 Flex-Foam Double-Sided Fusible

Uses or Tasks

Use in accessories, home décor, crafts, and bags (especially great for larger bags because it will hold the bag's shape).

Tips

- Make your own double-sided quilted yardage by fusing fabric to each side and do some quilting. Quilting can be simple, like walking-foot quilting.
- When fusing foam, it is very important to fuse from the fabric side. Test first! Place the fabric's wrong side to the fusible side of the foam. Place a damp press cloth over the top of the fabric, and with the iron set to cotton, press firmly (do not compress the foam) until the press cloth is dry. Test the bond.

Product/Type
Fusible fleece

Characteristics
Fusible fleece is a soft, spun polyester sheet that comes in varying thicknesses. The adhesive is either laminated or printed on its surface. Use this product when you want to add body to fabric to be used in pillows, pouches, and totes. It also adds a layer of softness to apparel.

Fiber Content
100% polyester

Limited List of Brand Names

- Pellon TP971F Fusible Termolam® Plus
- Pellon 987F Fusible Fleece
- Bosal 325 Fusible Polyester Fleece
- Bosal 426LF Single Sided Light Fusible Fleece

Uses or Tasks

When you want to save time, a fusible fleece will get you out of pinning and basting. Add fusible fleece to fashion fabric when a soft body and slight cushion is required. It can be quilted for texture.

Tips

- Add fusible fleece to fabric before machine embroidery to create loft in embroidered items. It has enough body to act as a stabilizer.
- When making pillows, fuse fleece to the inside cover before assembling and stuffing,
- When fusing fleece, the fusible side should be face up and the fabric should be fused over the top of the fleece.
- Use fusible fleece instead of heavy interfacing with upholstery fabrics that require stabilization—it will add stability but not stiffness and will be easier for you to do needlework.

Product/Type
Sew-in fleece

Characteristics
A soft, spun polyester sheet that adds full, lofty body to fabric. This product is great for fabrics that cannot be fused, such as delicate silks and metallic and textured fabrics.

Fiber Content
100% polyester

Limited List of Brand Names

- Pellon 988 Sew-In Fleece (packaged)
- Pellon 989 Sew-In Fleece (roll)
- Bosal 326 Sew-In Polyester Fleece

Uses or Tasks

Use for padded or quilted apparel and crafts.

Tips

- Sew-in fleece is very needle-friendly. Do a test swatch for padded quilting; you will get an idea of the effect it creates.
- Use for cutaway trapunto effects.

Product/Type
Insulated fleece

Characteristics
This is a polyester fleece that is needle-punched through a reflective Mylar® film that reflects heat or cold back to its source.

Fiber Content
100% polyester with reflective, metallized polyester film

Limited List of Brand Names
- The Warm Company Insul-Bright® 6345
- Bosal 364 Poly-Therm Heat Reflective Fleece
- Bosal 464 Poly-Therm Heat Reflective Fleece

Uses or Tasks
Use for projects that need to keep heat or cold in: pot holders, oven mitts, frozen food shopping bags, coffee cup sleeves, and lunch bags, to name a few.

Tips
- This type of material is not recommended for microwave use. (If you are looking for a product that will go in the microwave, look for a 100% cotton product specifically designed for microwaving.)
- Use two layers to make potholders to handle food above 400°F (200°C).
- The shiny side of the product is the side that needs to face the hot or cold item. If the product has the insulator inside the batting, then either side can face the hot or cold item.

Product/Type
Fusible cotton batting

Characteristics
This is a needle-punched cotton batting with a scrim (open-weave cotton fabric) to add stability while quilting. The fusible layer saves time by eliminating the need for pinning and basting.

Fiber Content
100% cotton

Limited List of Brand Names
- Hobbs Heirloom Premium 80/20 Fusible Cotton/Poly Blend Batting
- Bosal 4250 Duet Fuse Double Sided Fusible Batting

Uses or Tasks

Use for quilts, handbags, crafts, and accessories — any project that you would like to give a natural quilted texture.

Tips
- When fusing quilts, sandwich the back, fusible cotton batting, and quilt top. Clip them together with binder clips. Fuse from the center out to each edge.

Product/Type
Paper-backed fusible web

Characteristics
This fusible web is a bonded polyamide adhesive that is made into a "spun" fabric sheet on a paper backing that can bond two pieces of fabric together. Be sure that you follow the manufacturer's instructions—some have a temporary sticky back adhesive that can be used to position appliqué pieces.

Fiber Content
Resin adhesive

Limited List of Brand Names
- Pellon 805 Wonder-Under®
- Bosal 444 Fusible Splendid Web
- Therm O Web HeatnBond® or HeatnBond® Lite Iron-On Adhesive

Uses or Tasks
The uses for fusible web are limited only by your imaginations—here are just a few:
1. Hemming
2. Fusible appliqué
3. Make fabric fusible

Tips
- **Important!** Always protect your ironing surface with parchment paper or a Teflon sheet.
- Just starting out with machine appliqué? Test your stitch settings (length and width) on a scrap piece of fabric before you start. It is sometimes helpful to reduce your thread tension as well. Remember to make one change at a time until the desired look is achieved.
- There are a few different types; two examples are film (Therm O Web's HeatnBond) and web (Pellon's Wonder-Under). Always follow the manufacturer's instructions for fusing.

Product/Type
Unsupported fusible web

Characteristics
This is a fusible web that is not supported with a paper backing. Unsupported webs can be sheerer than paper-backed webs.

Fiber Content
Resin adhesive

- Mistyfuse

Uses or Tasks

Here are a few ways to use this type of interfacing:
- Fuse-baste quilts
- Layered appliqué projects
- Pre-fuse fabrics for use in cutting machines (die cutters or silhouettes)

Tips

- Follow the manufacturer's instructions. The biggest question concerning interfacing without a paper backing is: How do I use it? Lay the piece of web between two pieces of parchment paper and fuse. Let the piece cool. Gently peel away one layer of parchment. Place the parchment with the fusible over the design and trace. Fuse to the fabric and cut along the lines for a fusible appliqué.
- **Important!** Always protect your ironing surface with parchment paper or a Teflon sheet.

Product/Type
Fusible web tapes

Characteristics
There are various weights of fusible web tapes available that are cut to various widths for convenience. There are different uses—permanent, stretchy, very strong (no-sew), etc.

Fiber Content
Heat-sensitive adhesive

Limited List of Brand Names
- Therm O Web HeatnBond Hem Tape, Iron-On Adhesive
- Dritz Fusible Bonding Web Tape
- Clover Fusible Web Tape

Uses or Tasks
Use this product to bond fabrics together without stitching. These tapes are great for quick hemming projects.

Tips
- Follow the manufacturer's instructions for the correct iron temperature.
- Hemming curtains? Press the hem in first. Using a paper-backed roll, lay out the fusible interfacing between the hem and the curtain (removing paper as you go). Steam to fuse in place. Let cool and stitch.
- Make your own fusible bias tape for a custom look.
- Use hem tape to add trims to your projects—fuse the hem tape to the trim first, then remove the paper and fuse the trim to the project.
- **Important!** Always protect your ironing surface with parchment paper or a Teflon sheet.

Product/Type
Fusible tricot tape

Characteristics
Fusible tricot interfacing is cut into convenient rolls to
stabilize or finish seams on apparel, and to join batting
together for quilts.

Fiber Content
Heat-sensitive adhesive on tricot knit tape

Limited List of Brand Names
- Pellon ST-EK150 Easy Knit® Tape
- HEAT Press Batting Together
- Bosal 428-15 Batting Seam Tape

Uses or Tasks

This is a thin, flexible tape that easily contours to the profile needed. Use it to stabilize seams on knit garments and to join quilt batting together on a larger project.

Tips
- Follow the manufacturer's instructions. Align two straight edges of batting together, lay a strip of the interfacing tape over the join, and press to fuse.
- Finish the raw edges of the seams inside the garment without fusing, stitch to one side of the seam, then roll the tape to the other side and attach by fusing or stitching.
- **Important!** Always protect your ironing surface with parchment paper or a Teflon sheet.

Product/Type
Heat-moldable stiffener, sew-in or fusible

Characteristics
Very stiff interfacing that becomes soft and pliable with application of heat and steam. Can be sew-in or fusible.

Fiber Content
Nonwoven thermoplastic sheet

Limited List of Brand Names
- ◼ Bosal 490 Heat Moldable Stiffener 490
- ◼ Bosal 491 Heat Moldable Double sided Fusible
  Plus Stabilizer

Uses or Tasks
Cover with fabric, then mold into a shape. This product is
used in home décor projects, such as boxes or trays that
require a stable structure.

Tips
- ◼ If the stiffener is fusible, apply it to the fabric and
  either fuse or stitch in place.
- ◼ Use a Microtex sharp needle to pierce the material.

■ To mold, apply a damp press cloth on top of your finished piece (with the interfacing already attached) and heat at the highest temperature of your iron to soften the shape. Ensure that the shape is evenly heated before molding. Place the heated shape over a mold (for example, an inverted bowl) and let it cool. After your piece cools, it hardens again into the shape desired. If you don't like the result, just reheat and remold.

Product/Type
Heat-moldable batting

Characteristics
This soft, pliable nonwoven fabric is activated by heat. It can be formed and shaped into permanent shapes when exposed to steam, heat, or dry heat. It is durable for indoor or outdoor use and is extremely lightweight and breathable.

Fiber Content
Moldable resin set into a 100% polyester batting

Limited List of Brand Names
■ Bosal 494 Moldable Heat Activated Batting

Uses or Tasks
Quilt with it first, then heat for a hardened sheet. You can also create a design, and then activate it with your iron. You may stitch together slightly hardened sections as well. It should be noted that this material may shrink up to 15%, so it can be used to create an interesting texture. It's also great for costuming, and you can paint directly on it.

Tips
■ When heating, be patient. Place a damp press cloth over the area to be stiffened, and then apply your iron to the project. This can be done over a mold to create curves. A fabric steamer will work as well.
■ Heat-moldable batting will stick to itself and may be layered to achieve the required rigidity and density. A steam iron with a strong hand pressure will create an adequate bond between layers and provide more surface smoothness.

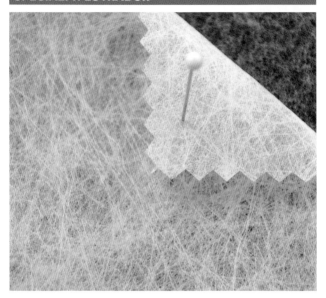

Product/Type
Lutradur, sew-in

Characteristics
This is a sew-in, spun-bonded, nonwoven interfacing used for sewing, crafting, fiber art, quilting, and scrapbooking.

Fiber Content
100% polyester

■ Pellon Lutradur®, 25g, 70g, and 100g

Uses or Tasks

Think of Lutradur as a cross between fabric and paper. It's mainly used in fiber art.

Tips

■ Iron no higher than the wool setting.
■ Paint on it (textile or acrylic paints).
■ Burn it for aged effects.
■ Layer it for art collages.

Product/Type
Steam-activated texturizing fabric, sew-in

Characteristics
This product is a steam-activated shrinking fabric that's used for "gathering" fabric for textured/smocked effects.

Fiber Content
100% polyester

Limited List of Brand Names

- Bosal's 500-18 Stitch & Seam
- Pellon Fabric Magic™

Uses or Tasks

Create beautiful textured effects to add to bags, art quilts, and craft projects.

Tips

- Simply sew to the back of your fabric and apply steam, and the fabric magically shrinks approximately 30%, creating a beautiful textured effect. After shrinking, the result is permanent.
- Do *not* iron before shrinking.

Product/Type
PUL fabric

Characteristics
A type of laminated fabric that is waterproof
and breathable.

Fiber Content
PUL stands for *polyurethane laminate*

Limited List of Brand Names

- Paintbrush Studio Fabrics PUL Solid 333-Color (various prints available as well)

Uses or Tasks

Use PUL fabric anywhere you need a waterproof, fluid-proof, breathable moisture barrier. Diaper covers, adult diapers, car seat protectors, changing pads, baby bibs, raincoats, laundry baskets, and makeup pouches are just a few examples.

Tips

- Do not use pins when assembling PUL pieces—use Wonder Clips or binder clips. This will prevent holes from ruining your waterproof fabric.
- Use a ballpoint or universal needle—not sharps. Use polyester thread *only*, as using cotton can cause wicking at the seam lines.
- Either use a Teflon foot or sew with the coated side against the feed dogs (laminated side down).
- Do *not* iron or dry clean.

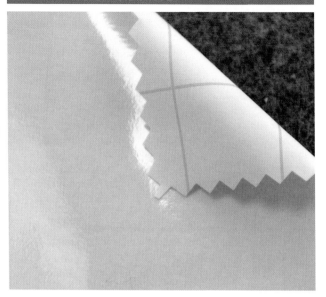

Product/Type
Iron-on vinyl, fusible

Characteristics
A flexible, water-resistant coating that you can fuse to any fabric to give it a protective coating.

Fiber Content
100% vinyl

Limited List of Brand Names

- Therm O Web HeatnBond 3902 Iron-On Vinyl (pack)
- Therm O Web HeatnBond 3926 Iron-On Vinyl (gloss bolt)
- Therm O Web HeatnBond 3927 Iron-On Vinyl (matte bolt)
- Pellon 100 Vinyl Fuse™ (gloss finish)
- Pellon 102-M Vinyl Fuse Matte

Uses or Tasks

Iron-on vinyl is great for making your own laminated fabrics—use for tote bags, placemats, and aprons, just to name a few.

Tips

- Prewash all materials before applying vinyl. Follow manufacturer's instructions for application. Allow to cool before sewing. Can be used on both sides of the project, bonding one side at a time.
- Use a Teflon foot to assemble. Do not use pins when assembling—use Wonder Clips or binder clips. This will prevent holes from ruining your waterproof fabric.
- Do *not* touch iron directly to vinyl.

Index of Uses

Category	Material	Clothing	Tailoring	Home Décor	Bags and Purses	Quilting/Art Quilting	Crafts
Interfacing	Woven interfacing	X	X	X	X	X	X
	Nonwoven interfacing	X	X	X	X	X	X
	Knit/tricot interfacing	X	X	X	X	X	X
	Quilter's grid			X	X	X	X
	Buckram		X	X	X	X	X
	Hair canvas		X	X	X	X	X
	Precuts for waistbands/purse straps	X		X	X		X
Stabilizers	Stabilizers for craft/home décor projects			X	X	X	X
	Decovil/Decovil light			X	X		X
	Sew-in foam stabilizer			X	X		X
	Fusible foam stabilizer			X	X		X
Fleece	Fusible fleece	X	X	X	X	X	X
	Sew-in fleece	X	X	X	X	X	X
	Insulated fleece			X			X
	Fusible cotton batting		X	X	X	X	X
Fusible Web	Paper-backed fusible web					X	X
	Unsupported fusible web					X	X
Tapes	Fusible web tapes	X					X
	Fusible tricot tape	X	X	X	X	X	X
Specialty	Heat-moldable stiffener				X		X
	Heat-moldable batting			X	X		X
	Lutradur			X	X	X	X
	Steam-activated texturizing fabric			X	X	X	X
	PUL fabric				X		X
	Iron-on vinyl				X		X

Resources

The following manufacturers and retailers make and/or sell the interfacings (and other "inners") listed in this guide.

- Bosal™ Foam, Fiber, Interfacing and Crafts (*www.BosalOnline.com*)
- ByAnnie's Soft and Stable™ (*www.ByAnnie.com*)
- Dritz® (*www.Dritz.com*)
- Fairfield™ (*www.FairfieldWorld.com*)
- HTC (*www.HTC-Retail.com*)
- Heat Press Batting Together™ (*www.HeatPressBatting Together.com*)
- June Tailor, Inc. (*www.store.JuneTailor.com*)
- Lazy Girl Designs (*www.LazyGirlDesigns.com*)
- Pellon® (*www.PellonProjects.com*)
- Quiltsmart® (*www.Quiltsmart.com*)
- Shades Textiles (*www.ShadesTextiles.co*)
- Superior® Threads (*www.SuperiorThreads.com*)
- Therm O Web (*www.ThermOWebOnline.com*)
- The Warm® Company (*www.WarmCompany.com*)

About the Author

Kristine Poor founded Poorhouse Quilt Designs in September 2006 after designing her Sampler Tote pattern as a gift. Since then, she has designed bags, bowls, banners, quilts, and ornaments. Kristine has a degree in Mechanical Engineering and a love of fabric and color; these seemingly conflicting pursuits have come together perfectly in her quilt design business. Kristine specializes in using unusual materials and sharing the results in her patterns (think of these projects as a "creativity booster shot"!).